W9-ART-474

7/09-71

WHALES

KILLER WHALES

JOHN F. PREVOST
ABDO & Daughters

Published by Abdo & Daughters, 4940 Viking Drive, Suite 622, Edina, Minnesota 55435.

Library bound edition distributed by Rockbottom Books, Pentagon Tower, P.O. Box 36036, Minneapolis, Minnesota 55435.

Printed in the United States.

Cover Photo credit: Peter Arnold, Inc.

Interior Photo credits: Peter Arnold, Inc.

Edited by Bob Italia

Library of Congress Cataloging-in-Publication Data

Prevost, John F.
 Killer whales / John F. Prevost.
  p. cm. — (Whales)
 Includes bibliographical references (p.23) and index.
  ISBN 1-56239-474-6
 1. Killer whale—Juvenile literature. [1. Killer whale. 2. Whales.] I. Title.
 II. Series Prevost, John F. Whales.
 QL737.C432P744   1995
 599.5'3—dc20   95-2750
                                                             CIP
                                                             AC

ABOUT THE AUTHOR
John Prevost is a marine biologist and diver who has been active in conservation and education issues for the past 18 years. Currently he is living inland and remains actively involved in freshwater and marine husbandry, conservation and education projects.

Contents

KILLER WHALES AND FAMILY

Killer whales are **mammals** that live in the sea. Like humans they breathe air with lungs, are **warm-blooded**, and **nurse** their young with milk. They are called killer whales because they hunt and eat other mammals.

Once killer whales were feared and seen as a threat to fishermen. Scientific studies have changed these old views. Killer whales are the largest members of the dolphin family. Like many of their cousins, killer whales are curious and **social**.

Killer whales are the largest members of the dolphin family.

SIZE, SHAPE AND COLOR

Males may reach a length of 31.5 feet (9.5 meters). The females are smaller and may reach 27 feet (8.3 meters).

Unlike other dolphins, the killer whale has a round face that does not have a long **snout**. The thick body supports a large **dorsal** fin that may reach 6 feet (1.8 meters) in height. The 2 spoon-shaped **flippers** are also large.

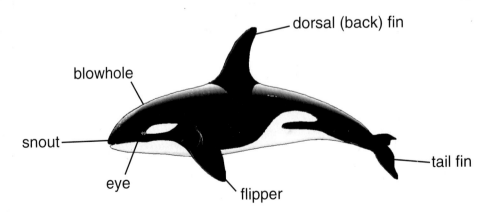

blowhole

snout

eye

flipper

dorsal (back) fin

tail fin

The killer whale's thick body supports a large dorsal fin.

Killer whales are white on their belly and under their head. There is also a white spot behind their eyes. They are black over their fins and back. A gray patch may also be found behind the dorsal fin.

WHERE THEY LIVE

Killer whales are found in oceans all around the world. They often swim within 500 miles (800 kilometers) of a coast. Unlike other whales, large killer whale groups are not divided by water temperature, distance, or **continents**.

There is only one killer whale **species**. Some groups will stay in one area if there is much food. Other groups will **migrate** to find food in seal **rookeries** or **spawning** salmon **estuaries**.

Killer whales are found in oceans all around the world. They will migrate to find food.

Killer whales are **social** animals. They often hunt in **pods** of about 30 whales. Larger **herds** of over 100 whales form when smaller pods join each other.

SENSES

Killer whales and people have 4 of the same senses. Their eyesight is good in and out of the water. Killer whales take an interest in their **habitat**. When boats approach, they will bob their head above the water surface to look at the boaters.

Hearing is their best sense. Because of its thickness, water passes on sound better than air. Many whales use sound to locate **prey**. By making loud clicks and whistles, killer whales hear the returning echoes and can tell what is around them. This is called **echolocation**.

HOW ECHOLOCATION WORKS

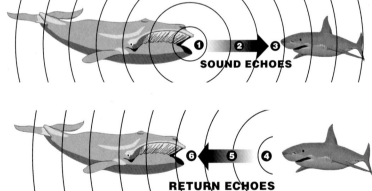

SOUND ECHOES

RETURN ECHOES

The whale sends out sound echoes (1). These echoes travel in all directions through the water (2). The sound echoes reach an object in the whale's path (3), then bounce off it (4). The return echoes travel through the water (5) and reach the whale (6). These echoes let the whale know where the object is, how large it is, and how fast it is moving.

Killer whales are curious creatures. They often surface to look at boaters.

Touch and taste are also well formed. In public **aquariums**, killer whales will touch new objects with their tongue. These **social** animals often touch each other to show feelings and to **communicate**. Killer whales do not have the sense of smell.

DEFENSE

Adult killer whales have no known enemies other than man. But humans have never made any money hunting killer whales. When threatened, a killer whale will dive and swim away.

The killer whale is a fearsome **predator**. Its large jaws have 40 to 48 large, cone-shaped teeth. These teeth curve inward to stop **prey** from pulling away. Other than another killer whale, there is nothing in the water that can challenge this predator.

When a killer whale feels threatened, it will dive and swim away.

FOOD

Killer whales eat fish, **squid**, birds, and other sea **mammals**. The **pod** pushes **prey** together and traps them. Then the killer whales feed together. Killer whales will also eat dolphins and **harpooned** whales.

Killer whales are often found near seal **rookeries**. They feed on seal adults and calves. Killer whales will beach themselves and scare seals and penguins to other pod members. Killer whales have never killed humans. But there have been some injuries.

Killer whales will feed on whales harpooned by whalers.
These whalers are cleaning a whale.

BABIES

A baby killer whale is called a **calf**. A calf is about 7 feet (2.2 meters) long at birth. Large sharks may attack it. But life in the **pod** offers the calf safety as well as **social** activity.

A calf needs its mother's care for at least the first year. It will stay within the pod until it becomes an adult at 10 years old. An adult male is about 23 feet (7 meters) long. An adult female is about 21 feet (6.5 meters) long.

When a killer whale is born, it is about 7 feet (2.2 meters) long and grows up to 16 feet (4.8 meters).

KILLER WHALE FACTS

Scientific Name: *Orcinus orca*

Average Size: 23 feet (7 meters) - males
21 feet (6.5 meters) - females
31.5 feet (9.5 meters) -
largest measured, a male

Where They're Found: In all oceans, but likes
coastal waters. May travel
into fresh water.

The killer whale.

GLOSSARY

AQUARIUM (uh-KWAIR-ee-um) - A building used for showing collections of living fish, water animals, and water plants.

CALF - A baby whale.

COMMUNICATE (kuh-MUH-nih-kate) - To exchange feelings, thoughts, or information.

CONTINENTS - The seven great masses of land on the Earth: Africa, Antarctica, Asia, Australia, North America, South America, Europe.

DORSAL (DOOR-sull) - Of, on, or near the back.

ECHOLOCATION (ek-oh-low-KAY-shun) - The use of sound waves to find objects.

ESTUARY (ES-tew-air-ee) - The mouth of a river where the current meets the sea.

FLIPPERS - The forelimbs of a sea mammal.

HABITAT (HAB-uh-tat)- A place where a living thing is naturally found.

HARPOON - A barbed spear used to kill whales.

HERD - A group of animals of the same kind.

MAMMAL - A class of animals, including humans, that have hair and feed their young milk.

MIGRATE - To travel from one region to another in search of food or to reproduce.

NURSE - To feed a young animal or child from the mother's breasts.

POD - A herd or school of whales or seals.

PREDATOR (PRED-uh-ter) - An animal that eats other animals.

PREY - Animals that are eaten by other animals.

ROOKERY - A place where animals gather to have babies and raise their young.

SNOUT - The part of an animal's head that extends forward and contains the nose, mouth, and jaws.

SOCIAL (SOE-shull) - Living in organized communities.

SPAWN - To lay eggs.

SPECIES (SPEE-seas) - A group of related living things that have the same basic characteristics.

SQUID: Marine animals related to the octopus that are streamlined in shape and have at least 10 arms.

WARM-BLOODED - An animal whose body temperature remains steady and warmer than the outside air or water temperature.

Index

BIBLIOGRAPHY

Cousteau, Jacques-Yves. *The Whale, Mighty Monarch of The Sea*. N.Y.: Doubleday, 1972.

Dozier, Thomas A. *Whales and Other Sea Mammals.* Time-Life Films, 1977.

Leatherwood, Stephen. *The Sierra Club Handbook of Whales and Dolphins*. San Francisco, California: Sierra Club Books, 1983.

Minasian, Stanley M. *The World's Whales.* Washington, D.C.: Smithsonian Books, 1984.

Ridgway, Sam H., ed. *Mammals of the Sea.* Springfield, Illinois: Charles C. Thomas Publisher, 1972.